D1564506

TUG

TUG

Stephen Todd Booker

TUG

STEPHEN TODD BOOKER

Wesleyan University Press
Published by University Press of New England
Hanover and London

Wesleyan University Press
Published by University Press of New England, Hanover, NH 03755
Printed in the United States of America
5 4 3 2 1
CIP data appear at the end of the book

Acknowledgments

The following poems have been published previously: "My Love . . . my greatest critic" [author's foreword], *Amanda Blue Poetry Magazine,* '80; " 'M,' " *Wascana Review* (Canada), '81; "Belief," *Wascana Review* (Canada), '82; "Lopping," *Kite,* '81; "Prospectus," *Kite,* '81; "Clarksville," *Tendril,* '82; "Asil Anom," *Croton Review,* '82; "A Reflection: Of The Sky On Wheat and The River," *The New Renaissance,* '82; "Book of Gad," *The New Renaissance,* '82; "Hopkinsville," *Bitterroot,* '82; "The Centrifugal Force of Orez," *Black American Literature Forum,* '83; "The Wrong Boy," *The Southern Review,* '90; "Spartacus in Metus," *New Delta Review,* '91; "In the Interest of Anthropology," *River Styx,* '92; "Requiem," *Timbuktu,* '91; "Escape to Kismet," *Seneca Review,* '91; "I, When A Bumblebee Bat," *Home Planet News,* '92; "Counting Backwards from Orez," *Psychopoetica* (England), '92; "Wisdom," *Bouillabaisse,* '92; and "Bhago's 'Revised' Revenge," *Scarp* (Australia), '92. The following poems currently are in press: "Democracy," in *Malcontent*; "The Pied Piper of Murderloin Downs," in *The Kenyon Review*; "Tug," in *The New Renaissance*; "Two Straws in the Wind of Mind," in *Psychopoetica* (England); and "Knowledge," in *ARG-Catazine.*

Illustrations are by I. D. Kline.

My Love . . . my greatest critic

She searches for a blue rose—
      (how amusing)—
in burr and briar thickets,
as I kick over the white picket fences
of a sluggish and servile consistency
concerning inspiration.

She reads me long into the night—
      yet upon awakening she has forgotten
      each one of the lessons I have
      taught her, via sleep.
It should seem a perfect pleasure,
      what with its chance of dreaming
     —(if not, a token justice),
a flawless confession, one she'll
          never comprehend.

I induce her to sit and listen as
I do my imitation of the shadowy
aftermaths of the last syllable
of a tern's shrill and whistling
moaning; the same, it is,
I tell her, is destined to forever
reverberate along the sunset's
hallways—lost forever,
      and then some . . .

That this book exists
owes a great deal of thanks to the following people—

Betty & Richard Vogh
Johnese & Godfrey Lennon • Denise Levertov
Catherine McGrath • Page Zyromski
Lenny Silveira • Susan Swartwont • James E. Coleman, Jr.
Marge Simon • the Bruderhof kids
& many others

Special thanks to
E. Tony ('Castro') Valdez,
whose curiosity pulled Tug *out of mothballs.*

CONTENTS

TUG

Belief

How like the ideal gift, what next
To his world of twelve years was apt to flood
The psyche with fifty xs of wonders, distortions
Across a channel previously forded by a tunnel.

"Ah, yes," he said, "I am now sovereign
Of more than I had upon arriving." This was
During an era when ligustrum hedges
In six by six square plots determined
Which houses on the block were beautiful,

And ivy, climbing and tumbling from every windowpot,
Acted as an inviolable buffer—after trolleys that ran on
Tracks (embedded in cobblestones) were replaced by buses.
A while before the stones were pried and sold as pets.

A hook and ladder
Would come thundering out of an engine company,
The firemen clinging to her like pilotfish.
A cop in the rain wore a bright yellow slicker
So no cars'd jump the curb to run him over for kicks,
And a church in the neighborhood rang bells
Heard clear down to the navy yard.

The Centrifugal Force of Orez

In deference to ourselves,
because we are the dominant will-brain,
from a seed

blown into this grotto of bedrock
and stayed,
we've built a kingdom from the unknown.

And it's here
we expect redwood to sprout
like errant hairs upon shew-bread—

for those who ooh and ah their forebears,
who routinely assemble to take in lovers
swapping trivial vows—

the exterior strata—
as if they're an obvious transparency
jogging on a trampoline of quicksand.

Democracy

A dandelion seed of woman,
She, the daughter hated by her own
Mother and sisters for having two sons—
Because perhaps too she wasn't so alone
As to agree that black men were evil,
Each an agent of Satan, the devil;
Nor could she revel in the slaughter
Of her brothers, and became outspoken
In refusing to speak ill of anyone.
For that she was *persona non grata,*
And even mentioning her name was shunned.
It probably helped to kill my Mother,
Never being let back into the warmth
Of what should've been a familial sun.

Many another dandelion seed,
While buffeted by the four winds' reprise,
Will invariably still crave the love
Of her own blood-kin, and suffer the need
To be needed by them—so what if lies.
And that is the way she gets dealt the card
Filling her cupboard with nothing but lard,
As her siblings maintain their faith in fate,
Their girths increasing along with their hate—
Prosperity telling them they have guts,
They telling themselves nigguhmen need nutts.
Across town, Sis will live by candlelight,
And chicken-delight, or take-out chinese.
She will teach her sons to pray on their knees.

Sometimes allmotherfuckinnight she prayed;
Or, she'd writhe in pain, unable to sleep,

Fighting a migraine she had had for days.
In the morning, she'd be a quantum leap
Ahead of her time, and again her long,
Go-getter legs would have her up, swinging—
She, the very embodiment of *strong*.
Once dead, you would have sworn by the keening
Of her sisters and Mother she was loved.
Once cremating her, that mission was scrubbed.
In posthaste time, both sisters and Mother
Were squabbling over her meager estate.
One son claimed it his by law; the other
Quietly watched them dicker and debate.

Wisdom

We kids did chase and stone a goofy square.
None of us knew the dude. A lapsed rabbi? . . .
Maybe . . . none of us cared. Shoeless, he ran
Through Crown Heights, and on into East New York;

Brownsville; and, finally, to East Flatbush,
Bobbing like a jettisoned cork, howling.
For the trailing fumes of the shitty aura
He always wore, we christened him Tarzan.

As to what his harsh Yiddish curses meant,
Or the sonorous Hebraic prayers
For clemency, again, none of us cared,
Not with our summer vacations spent

In a quandary over something to do
Besides spotting him limping through the park,
Going someplace, or just out on a lark.
Once, after we had followed him for hours,

We ventured into a land that sported
Sculpted hedgerows, trees, and manicured lawns,
And white faces oozing hatred and scorn;
Whereas, little black sambo jockey-guards,

Steady, hard and fast, and pink flamingos,
Were attending to their balancing act
Before the quaint, white houses that we passed.
And damned if those people didn't have holes,

Right in the sidewalk, down to the sewers
Or down to hell, holes for garbage *and* trash;

And the air there was honeysuckle fresh
And blessed with an oceany kind of smell.

The more we walked the giddier we got,
Clean forgetting about the Jew we stalked.
Lapsed rabbi? . . . howling hippie? . . . Whichever.
Jumping the subway without a token,

We kids hurried back to our own hometurf,
Back to the things we cared about and knew.
And you know what . . . ? It was good to be home.
It was good to have homes, and shoes.

"M"

———

Her man-cubs are such an armload
Teething on plastic rings, as from
Lips bruised by their due of
Mechanical, insipid kissing,
Menthol is the cigarette. Her man is a
War.

She's still likely your redoubtable
Fortress of shopping bags, and eyes of
Molten, honest appraisal—to the
World—and against the
Quills of civilian
Write off.

Lopping

I learned rows of cabbage
Mustard greens. In prison,
Downsouth. Privet

Ilex aquifolia.
The rank of skunk.

In a fetal posture
You go from head to head,
Lopping.
The heads don't perk up or
Cringe they see you coming.
And just how they get away
With a lot of history and
More of today you got to
Tell me so I'll know.

Pass it around. Pass it around
In a circle of men stripped
Bare to the waist.
Going barefoot is optional.

Pass a head of cabbage.
"Look at the worms!" one will cry out.
"Look at the worms *inside of the head!*"
So shouts another.
Look at both. I've learned.

Clarksville

1.

At what he is so poignantly described was within
The expanses of timber, I looked, and I
Listened, to the accent of one trained in
Falsity—to such an extent recital
Gave rise to not the minutest tinge of flush
Upon his haggard jaw—
No more than you'd hear tell of a mockingbird
Agreeing to give a commentary on his own
Deception, his defensive coloration,
His birthright.

2.

He had said the shortening can
Contained the best damn shine everwas,
And he asked me again, "You want some?"
I declined, as I'd done five miles back.
"Suit yourself," he said, and took a swig.
My reply was that I would, suit myself.
He re-covered the can with a plastic lid
And started in where he'd left off,
Pointing or gesturing to no specific place
On my side of the road,
To scenes of great battles.

3.

He had me to know he was one of the last
Survivors of the 'grand ruckus,' the only

Real-war there was. And so, of course,
As he put it, he was an authority on
The charges heaped in layer upon counter-
Offensives, tactical retreats, and the
Nightly filibuster of artillery bartering
For the crack of caps propelling lead balls
In a direct path to anything moving. . . .
"And we never know'd what all was lurkin' 'hind
Boulders or up in the 'nolias"—"'Stay alert!
No smokin' on the line.' Those were passwords."

4.

"It's right dandy," he said. ". . . sure you can't use
A nip?" He held the can out to me and
Floored the gas pedal as I gave in to his
Pestering. And I couldn't help but adjourn
What doubts I'd had about the elixir's potency
And taste. "This is pretty decent stuff, old man.
What's in it?" Our eyes met for the first time.
I saw then, in the bluest of eyes set in
Red, a malevolence, an evil I haven't seen
Since but am relieved to know where
It resides. His birthright.

Asil Anom

And to think, this started as a poem
About mitosis inside of a crystal,

About my gliding through an ugly room
Of a foldaway cot and mirrored bureau

And pausing before a bogus panel
In the bathroom wall, or about pages

In a book of riddles about places
A fly may go to in winter turning brown,

And why the tabbytom
Let inside some thirty years ago

Burys a hairball behind the rosebush!

The Pied Piper of Murderloin Downs

Residing in the cave nextdoor to me,
Ununderstood, practically de-eyed,
Toothless, insensate, and ready
With an infectious smile, is a killer.
Divvying up his meals at chowtime,
Sacrifices are laid out for mice, he says
To save them hunting in our cells at night.
Rats visit him occasionally; and he is
Their Messiah too. Birds (namely,
Sparrows), he kills. Daily;
He bends staples into teensyweensy hooks,
Baits them with balls of bread and . . .
There is a seldom-observed
Type of gagging or death-rattle
That is a horrific opera . . .
A churning puff of dusty brown feathers
Going berserk, dervishly jiggabooing,
Going over the edge of the tier's catwalk,
Gone noiselessly down to meet the first floor . . .
And there is
On one end of a length of thread,
And quivering, that last, precious tweet-tweet
On the catwalk,
Fresh meat for the mice.

Serendipity

Conjured in smoke by my island brother:
A dab of nubbed-in sailor's sunshine,
Lobster-red and overhead; forever-watched
Youth, sprouting like fertilized weeds; higher,
Poised, in a terraced garden in Paradise, you,
Selling orchids after culling the fattest ram
Out of your small herd to feed their soldiers.
Curiously, this image is no glossier now,
Used as a recruiting poster, than glaring
Moons were then spotlights over the guilty:
Signals are no more less apt to having
Kiltered themselves mixed: it is a given.
Askew, even on an updraft, the view is everything.

Spartacus in Metus

If there had been something
Tattooed on him while in the womb
Of his dimpled past, or during
And after the numbing experiences
He had run amok through—

When cigarettes laced with heroin
Was what lifted him out of the fear
That had held him fast— he had,
By the time of his exposure to me,
Lost it; and, he'd lost himself

And everything else, by his own
Grinning and bearing it shuffle,
And also in his fuss to be and do
Everything for everyone. So what
Wry, sardonic ideogram had he? . . .

Something selected from out of the blue?
Angels or eagles, owls or butterflies?
Or a pair of grimacing, winged dragons?
Well, what he did have was the residue
Of the word "Mother" on his left eyelid;

And it was obvious that it had been
Successfully abraded down to a scar
Bracketed by just the empty quotes.
Plus, where no collar could ever
Hope to hide them, there were

Dots tattooed on the sides of his neck,
While ". . . cut along the dotted line . . ."

Was festooned around his throat. It is
The consensus, all-time wolf-ticket
To advertize how tough one thinks he is;

But, not even his two extended tours
As a bush-monkey, as an infantryman
Humping the boondocks of Vietnam,
Hacking off ears to confirm a bodycount,
Could have prepared him for prison life.

Thus it is no paradox: hoorahs get impaled
Upon a sigh: he begged me to be his
War-daddy, offering his Rolex as a dowry,
A steady ration of satisfaction, and his
Disability check, to be my jailhouse wife.

I, When A Bumblebee Bat

Only twice in twelve long years
Has the Self in me transformed
To weighing less than a cent,
And blended with the evening,
Or heard ringing in my ears,
Or seen a star do its thing,
Umbrellaed aloft on air.
Swooping into a huge swarm
Of mosquitos and gnats, there,
On velvety wings, I went
Gliding and eating until
Chilled to my buoyant marrow,
Convinced not to eat my fill,
To leave some for tomorrow.

Prospectus

1.

Outdoor cages in the dead
of winter lie agape, the
mouth of a victim, compound eyes
of the clearest yet
indefinable color.

One brash bear in a coat of shag
stands on hindfeet

just like a man does each day
of his life. He laps out
at the falling snowflakes;

his tongue is as big
as any decent novel.

2.

The cages inside are lined up in
single file. Something is dead
or dying here where redhots and
gravel, malted milkballs,
and sections of navel oranges have
been fed to panthers and lions.

In the corners of their eyes
tears have congealed to jell
then petrified.

There is no drumroll.
No barbershoppole-painted stand
to take a stand upon and groan.
There's no show of teeth, and
not one paw is raised in defiance.

3.

Outside again there is an old man
on a bench.

The grey squirrel is his pal.
They both have their butts on
the snowcovered planks of wood.

They carry on a conversation
older than the oldest tree
in the park, older than the park.

Two Straws in the Wind of Mind

1.

An enlightened, well-travelled friend of mine,
Infinitely intuned with what will be,
Neglected to consider that maybe I
Today can use the future's scoop on me.
And he spun how busy he was today:
Phased-in and being the guy who won't
Offset the suspense of a life of delays,
Especially by warning those who don't
Trim down the odds of being brought to task,
Sails tattered and their flapping clearly heard,
Tacking in the wind as if signal flags,
Radically encoding these vital words:
'Arrives one poet . . . departs one prophet . . .
Washed-up, washed-out . . . know it or knock it.'

2.

Aren't both of them targets of caprice,
Natural prey for people to slay without
Alternatives, then themselves just corpses
To prove what a belief can't and doesn't?

Having rearranged the final tally,
Every soothsayer is an easy find—
Matter-of-fact poets too are like that:
Anticipated coiled in a haystack.

Menace is their proverbial needle,
Apparent, yes, but difficult to lose,
Resolutely sucking them dry. Is it

Asking too much to suggest that before
Nature is injected with a dose of you,
Advice be found that you can heed and use?—

Then shared with friends, as you have received it—
Handicapping little else . . . and bet on
Answers loaded, shook, and rolled by yourself?

A Reflection: Of The Sky On
Wheat and The River

You see, I too have eaten off a boring,
Chipped realestate, dinnerware upon checkered
Cloth that marks time. And from pure thought
A wonderous drug surged pell-mell through my
    arteries,
Like in minarets in the classical sense,
Fashioned after the design of termite mounds,
The Azan in morse code pulsing along spiral
Stairwells. Tedium doubled as creation myth
   and the theory was propounded

   nothing was or is. It's a pill to swallow,
As now I do. I've created from vapors mostly
Space for a factory where salamanders
Are the employees. I have them working
Non-stop in crayon, novas and suns in bibs

   and bonnets, half mine, half yours.
Tawny, rustic, amber waves that are
Transformed into fibers, and
Corollas made of daisies, tears, and icons
Were invented by them for the uninitiated.

The One No One Will Hear

This is the bullet that sizzles, and does
Sound like the crack of doom as it
Gulps down and swallows every matter
Whole, and has nobody to answer to.

Souls with kitetails streaming behind them
Bodies that have failed and are useless
To all concerned, and legions of deadheads,
Live again, it is said, after mourning

But themselves; for they live between cross hairs
Lives burnt like leaves racing in their falling
To the ground. This bullet will sound them out.
Brag, they have, assured of how fast they are;

And they laugh like cheerful skulls—just like you
Laugh—hoeing a row that is no different—
About six feet below the either-or.
It is you who this bullet is for. Amen.

and fear gripped me a...

the wet succulence

surrounding me

and binding me in from all sides

and doing so
I did taste

I erased away some

This taste... It's also be another feeling...

tasting

and

I couldn't ↑

Me; I, in the sweet mishmash

corn

in some sure a

And then —

a poem

Book of Gad

We're no longer exactly cognizant of late,
smitten by noxious fumes of nostalgia—
facing another ill-gotten sunrise while
bars and grilles in limbo forge on,

filled with the florescence of optimism. But we do
know there're those who are right now riddling
the once definitive, the glyphos,
into a wordplay on stardom—

ministering to a tenth cup of coffee in
an all-night diner, saying
they can recover from a habit,
literally, overnight,

thinking they can distinguish
between rap, which is superlative, which is a
tryst with dogma, which is the laughtrack.
It's a lie.

In the Interest of Anthropology

It's necessary, exercising the memory
Even with the off-color or minor-key
Occurrences that can be as ubiquitous
As ants at a picnic, and with stuff
Like the expression on a friend's face as we
Spied his mother going into the poolroom
On DeKalb Avenue, always in the shadow
Of the State Theatre marquee.

She'd gone there to collect her man,
To stop him from spending his payday,
To distract him from gambling and losing
At nineball. It's necessary, how you noticed
How his face was a motif with eyeballs
That were filmed over, and yet they possessed
A subdural glint, which in retrospect
Is reminiscent of slum jewelry.

It sticks with me as I hit the rack,
Even now, in nineteen and eighty-nine,
In sub-zero Florida,
Decked out in the full bivouac regalia
Of everything I own,
Plus what the State's Dept. of Corrections
Has loaned me—the necessariness
Of acknowledging certain memories

(What with boll weevil and bolshevik crackerdom
Marching to the same drummer,
Performing the same drill:
Genepooling because they are the minority
Here on the third planet). And it continues

Sticking like the craziest glue:
My friend's mother,
Whose name was Mary,

On the receiving end of a beating
With a cue stick, her man
Doing a Hank Aaron on her noggin until
Dislocating his arm. And she kept her cool,
Kept getting up.   She had defied the odds.
Lazy, ho-hum Saturdays should not
For these discoveries be: Mary
Could tolerate a heap of brutality,

Where later on down the line
That dingleberry man of hers
Would, when ensconced in a different woman's biography,
Wake up one ordinary Saturday morning
Falsetto and foaming lye through his attitude.
There's a braindead part of me getting antsy
Knowing that the truth sometimes
Becomes an open sore. But it's necessary,

Remembering memories, ants, and faces,
And a fist of a man blasted from dreaming
Of chalking up a bloody cue stick to recoup
Wine money after losing a week's salary,
A week's groceries. Telling myself
It's relevant and can move mountains,
I've whetted my memories sharp. I bide my time.
The movie: The Manchurian Candidate.

Escape to Kismet

Leaving means to the hills,
To the rocky hills above Kui,
Whose lush plateaus (that come
In cherry and bamboo flavors)
Provide her with a shield.

And her innocence is her armor,
Or it was. But what's a guy to do . . .
When indoctrinated to the ways of a buck,
What a dollar can buy, for keeps,
And how by dint of its wherewithal,

Its capacity to wound or massage,
It can in perpetuity rent anything it wants?
Nothing is sacred. No thing is untouchable.
Not one sin is so cardinal as to be
Beyond the indulgent sweep

Of its olive-drab tentacles; however,
Not in the rocky hills above Kui,
Whose lower slopes are a sumptuous muck,
A quagmire of divergent motives,
Gripped in the thrall of consummating

An opportunity. Not for any price was
Her magic *when* for sale (when
There came an intrusive tapping
On the floor, under the black Kimono
That had—like an indigo waterfall—

Slid from her ripe body like blight
From a piece of exotic fruit); yet if the words
To your own magic spell were intoned

Correctly, without a hitch in the delivery
Or averting the eyes—you my main ho . . .

My ichiban geisha ho—the tap, tap, tap—
That meant zip it and hit the door,
As in a general sense Taps means
Get your shit and split, scram—
Could tap on forevermore, a backdrop-backbeat

To the goings-on in the mirror on her ceiling,
On this side of the upstairs floor. Afterwards,
She'd say "You no go. Stay with Miko allnite.
Mamasan no thinky you here . . . she think another
Skivvy Joe shortime pushypushy

And him try for second cumshot free . . . she hear bed
Like we fight . . . I go tell soon it you and I
No more worky tonite. You stay . . . O.K. . . . ?
Tomorrow we go to Kui, horsebackride in hills,
Maybe pushypushy under goodluck kumquat tree.

Next we go to Naha, to dopeman, buy Buddhagrass,
Go to cinema, then back here . . . bang allnite,
Have bigfun like alltimes do. I play slavegirl.
She be cherrygirl . . . she do allthings for you."
O.K. So you've never left. Because leaving means—

Not in the decades of days of nights
Of minutes dreamt in tenses,
While like the bereaved father of a raindrop,
Spilling and keeping right on spilling,
Until the riptide of a zillion unborn tears

Slams into the beard of your musing *what if*—
You'll oneday have to admit to yourself
You left her without as much as a faretheewell.
And leaving means you would if you could
Have to return to her and love just as much

What she probably still will sell.

Counting Backwards from Orez

Tick-tock-tick . . . but not so brief
As to have to slid by unobserved,
Are those times when bluffing snakes—
When they were disguised as mankind—
Sympathized with us for settling
For the dust that we deserved.

Then the snakes slithered away,
Incredulous and disgusted,
Their raspy passing muffled
Under one man's presuming
That not even the gods of dust
Ever gave a good goddamn.

And though this man seemed to be
Of a pious bent, it was he,
Who, beseeching all of the gods
To bend low their receptive ears,
Would bathe the feet of any god
In a sea of gall and tears.

"For what are you bruising me?"
He'd begin his wily questions,
Using the same guileful ruse
With which he would seduce and dupe
Other snake-men, the fishes,
Birds, and beasts. "I demand answers . . ."

"Are you crushing me for my
Shedding the laying on of hands,
Or for my engineering
Their belated release of me?

Or is it my untimely undoing
Because of my proving that you
Are not what gets us men through the night—
Though granted the sanctuary
Of a painless end or the haven
Of a few seconds' relief?"

It happens today—tock-tick-tock—
As soon as people are dressed—
Dolled up in invisible scales,
Our family crest engraved
With the motto 'In Us We Trust.'
We are mauled to death by stress.

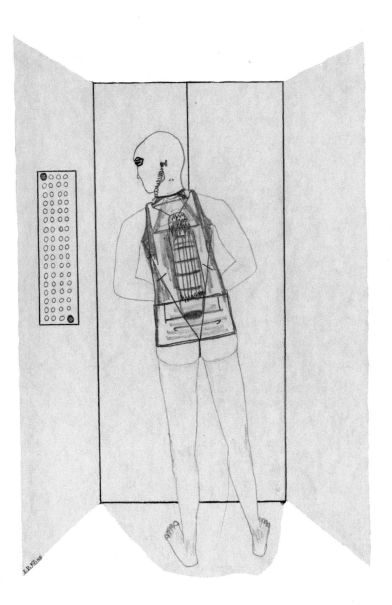

Bhago's "Revised" Revenge

Scorching a course through splendor,
Often having to get down and thump,
Scars on me are a testimony to my

Having not been an on-the-job trainee
Yearning for an annuity or a grant.
Slashes and raggedy, healed gashes,

Interlined in stitches that appeal
To the inquisitiveness in everyone,
Leap and strut on me like a legend

On an addled map. And I have one that
Offers no leverage and no exit to anyone
Kinky or noticeably crude; and a few,

Measured by using inkblots, can recall
Entire grids of displaced blame and blues,
Inlaid with deep moods and lacerations,

Not always a provocation with payment due
Those who tamed me as a child. And take my mitts . . .
Had they not deflected some of the hits

Envisioned as darts aimed at my spar,
Foxfire would be the lamp in my box—
And I'd not be here to answer the factored-in

Critics who, entrapped by the fury
Eking out of my pen, are in no position to deny
Identifying me with pens and poetry now.

Albeit, I have mastered their lingo and language,
Muscling my turgid bow through a karmic storm,
Yawl, that is me, scudding the crested swells

Of seas where the I of me was seldom allowed.
Uncharted carnivals of flesh, these waters are,
All aghast at my passing their frigid tests.

Naturally, the glittering haul of golden nuggets
Dazzling inside of my favorite forward hold—
Yardstick to what is thought to be the rest

Of my obsession to stay outside their reach—
Usually does more than impeach or reprove
Attacks on or to my state or peace of mind,

Reacting by not responding in kind but by opening
Embrasures whose inky, grapeshot repartee
Makes like a multiplicity of musketry and moves

Every dissenter out of the picture and out of my way,
Jibing my somewhat cryptical, griotic intent
Alee or not conforming to an Orphic bent.

Say what . . . ? . . .
. . .

The Wrong Boy

When the heel of my left foot
Stomped down, grinding the top of his
On the accelerator, his countenance,
Florid to begin with, was suddenly
Ashy, pallid, and drooping like a hound.
He started shaking, his bottom lip
Trembling. He wasn't smiling anymore.

Easing the pressure on his foot and the pedal,
I let the Ford slow to a manageable speed,
And still with the heel of my army shoe
Piggybacking his booted instep, I down-
Shifted the car and casually steered
With my left hand, turning
Off the highway and onto a dirtroad.

We drove in silence, the car
Jolting across bumps in the road,
Pebbles pinging up into the underchassis,
The nickel-plating on the gun in my right hand
Catching the waning sun just so . . . so pretty . . .
Kentucky is nice that time of year. In his lap,
His stubby fingers were clasped tightly together.

His knuckles were as white as they'd ever get,
As long as skin was on them. A fat blue vein
Wiggle-wobbled on the back of one hand.
I said, "Brake . . . ," and he applied the brakes,
"Out . . . ," and he exited with his hands
Over his head. If he had turned and faced me,
He'd have gotten slapped with the gun.

Kicked, he went sprawling, curled into a ball
And reached behind himself to rub his ass,
Whimpering and whining "O,Lawdy . . . dear, sweet
Jesusgod . . ." For good measure he wore a good
Ten or more swift kicks in the midriff and shortribs,
Plus a helping of the rebuilt gun on an elbow,
On the funny bone. "Shut up . . . ," he shut up.

He couldn't very well dry up altogether,
So there he was, stretched on the ground, crying,
While I turned the car off and got my gear
From the backseat. Returning to him,
I laid my duffel bag down a few feet away
And sat myself down. Cocking the pistol,
I stared down its sights into his eyes.

The bore of the big .45, I'm sure
Because I'd look into it myself
To see how it felt, probably looked so big . . .
So big that his mind either went blank
Or somersaulted, trying to cope with pictures
Of being sucked into the gun barrel
And meeting a bullet coming out . . .

So big and black, dispassionate . . .
It was a night sky devoid of stars
He knew how to find his way home by. Coughing,
He threw up moonshine and bile, his dentures
Landing in the puke. Switching hands with the gun,
I got the roll of tape and the pen-sized flashlight
From the inside breast pocket of my uniform.

I quickly tore off two strips
And taped the penlight to the gun barrel.
It was dark by then, pine trees way to the west
Having dragged the sun down, the humming
Of bugs and frogs croaking a steady drone

Like the audience in a theater when a cartoon
Or a coming attraction is not what they came for.

"It must've been a bitch to do war
Being born twenty-five years after Appomattox."
I aimed the light between his eyes.
"Several of your drinking buddies posed
A hassle, but I've tracked you all now. Fact is,
Your cousin Albert described you to a tee.
You're like hunting hot in the desert."

He sniffed and blinked. "You knew Al . . . ?
Why then he sured a told you I'm a fibber.
I ain't old enough to been in no Civil War, boy.
I only gets carried away. Mister . . . I been a buff
Of that war since I was a child. Please . . .
I didn't mean you no harm. I give rides
To hitchhikin' GIs all the time and jokes with 'em."

I stood and snapped the light off,
Uprighted my duffel bag, undid the hasp,
And fished around inside for what I needed.
Some coins clinking together in his overalls
Informed me that he'd braced himself, probably
To try and make a run for it. "Go on . . .
So I can catch you and cut your hamstrings."

My eyes being adjusted to the darkness,
I saw him lie back down, and with a sigh,
He said, "O, God, what'd I do . . .?"
It's peculiar how each had inquired of God
What he'd done instead of me. . . . The moon
Squirted from behind the clouds. A cool breeze
Brought with it the smell of tilled earth.

Sitting down, I snapped the light on again,
Placing the gun in my lap so that its light
Was again on him. Unzipping the leather case

38

I'd removed from my duffel bag, I took out
My old family Bible and set it aside.
Leaning closer to him, I said,
"Stick out your paws, Johnny Reb. . . ."

Faster than a rodeo cowboy can rope a calf,
I had his wrists bound to his ankles with tape.
He didn't get to query anyone this time
Because I planted a kick in his mouth
That knocked him out. When he came to,
Hours later, blubbering, spitting clots of blood
And the few real teeth he had, I opened the Bible.

Picking the pistol up, too, I scooted
Right close to him so he could see me
Thumbing through the Good Book, and so I
Could see his eyes widen in wonderment.
They had all worn that same questioning,
Quizzical sort of look near to where just
Before when I cured them, of everything.

Then, same as I'd done with the others,
I let the old, faded photograph fall out
Of the Bible like I didn't know it was there.
"Oh," I said, "what's this?" Picking it up,
I angled it so the light would be centered on it.
He broke wind, sputtering, spraying, dumping
A load in his overalls, and tried squirming away.

"What's the matter? You a party pooper?
You better funkyworm on back here by me
Before I introduce you to Mr. Knife.
I mean now." . . . Of course I had to
Grab a cuff of his pants and drag him back.
"Now . . . open your eyes and look at it. . . . That is
You, isn't it? In the Rebel-style cap and sheet?

This is you, huh? . . . Holding the jar of liquor? . . .
You're about as merry as Christmas . . . looks like it.

You look to be in your prime too, eh? A full man . . ."
I had the photo inches from his face. "Truth is,
You were twenty-four years of age and were
A member of the Ku Klux Klan. . . . The klavern
You were in was started by cousin Al, true?

And though you did have a cover name,
Calling your social club the Loyal Order of the
Brotherhood of the South—Lobos for short—
You were the same klan as ever.
Don't matter the wolf emblem on your robe
Or your Rebel cap acey-deuced to the side . . ."
His breathing was labored, tears flowing freely.

"That other gentleman—the one in the tree—
Or rather, the one up in the 'nolia—
He was married to my great-grandmother. . . .
His young wife, this same great-grandmother of mine,
She left this Bible with their daughter, and her
To hers, and she to me. . . . This photograph came
With the Bible, and a story you and I know.

This photo is in books about lynchings, too,
Klan murders and how punks like you got away."
I waved the photo under his nose.
"My great-grandmother's husband . . ." From my pocket,
I took out my Zippo and put its flame to a corner
Of the old photo. "By the bye, my grandfather was—is—
Half-white . . . But we know which, don't we?"

The moon was a marshmallow being absorbed by
A blanket of cotton candy. The wilted, charred
Remnants of a photo lay on the ground,
Beside it a burned book. The beam from a penlight
Surveying them for the last time drew
A small moth to the fire that had been. It
Fluttered in the thin shaft of light. So pretty

Hopkinsville

Save for when a jot or a tittle
Of graffiti was on the bark of "Take ten!
Ten yards apart!" they displayed no zeal,
No concern; yet the bugler's dirge sounded,
"Forward! Forward!" the same frothy slogan
On both sides, and everyone dropped
As cannonshot plummeted to earth
Like spherical, heartless anvils . . . death
Pacing its cage of unpredictability . . .
That eventual coalescing of fear,
Desire, and better-judgement . . .
Then the startled-bristled soldier
Stirred to by the prick of a bayonet.

Knowledge

With reason a tutor not for hire,
I shall endeavor to show you how

To solve the mystery of who it is
Has inherited the lake of fire.

Rounding figurative strokes of six
Espied as being possible clues,

Aren't you tired of all such abuse
Seizing you in its taboo, its pit

Of sin and guilt, or catechism,
Nurtured by conjecture and dispute,

And allegedly the best rebuke
To dump on men like me, in prison?

Unread the book. Count that the leaven
Tossed from me to you for free, unmixed,

Ostensibly, to unveil the six
Responsible for nailing the seven.

Now you can peek behind the mirror
On the hidebound wall of your despair.

There shouldn't be a single thing there
Fearsome or breathing heavily, or—

Oh, wait. . . . Here is my vaunted wisdom,
Referent, to say the least . . . unsealed,

Highfalutin, and seen as revealed
Imagery sprung from intuition,

Roving an enciphered alphabet
Epitomized by but two letters,

Lest erudition be in fetters:
"Perdition" is a proof, not a threat.

Requiem

I.

Jacked up from its grip in a tin of salve,
Three-fifths of which was oil, I had a wick
Of cloth that when lit it was like a lance,
Defending against the spots and the blips
That would try to envelop my world. And,
From behind no stiffer front than was that
Threadbare yet functioning bulwark of light,
While fighting off sleep, I did shape by hand
Dozens of worlds, draped in a kind of mist,
Bounding from my silence and taking flight:
To a world apart from where the rumor
Of a treaty between freedom and fraud,
By and large, betrayed my sense of humor
To be a penny-wise, pound-foolish whore.

But not always taken for granted, I've flown
From pale mouths and lips through paler claws,
Thrown up by groupie iconoclasts,
And that rare editor, drunk on cheap wine.
And then like the cigarette that causes a cough,
After I was puffed on and reviewed,
The jongleurs of an oblique critique
Had me metaphored into something paused,
Although my aim was straight and true. How
Very sweet I would be seen as being
If willing to drop what takes guts to cite—
Sweeter still, never trying to juggle
Being both the messenger and message
Received, when the hunter's moon is bright.

Nevertheless, flying like a bird,
Or off and running, I am at my best—
At variance with baseball poems
And anecdotal axioms about
The bedevilling fragrance of swine,
Hunkering down in the perfect ambush
Underneath my seeming not to know
Which niche in spaceless time or timeless space
Is mine—accepting risks and bucking
Rules pertaining to what is politic
And safe for me to say and to write—
As if setting about upon a loom
To weave a false itinerary
Of where I've been and am going to.

2.

Down . . . down through the wet chute
Of gloom, as if a maverick torpedo
After missing its mark, or a meteor
Leaving a rarefied contrail of gases
And baubled expletives,
Rising upward to the light
That pierces the dark, is my daisy chain of words,
Sent to the cleaners, in swift descent,
Slipping into an eternal night
Because that's how an accommodationist's
Fears are assuaged (although his ears
Go Pop! like in some nebulous vacuum anyway).
His is the spent poetics of fish bait,
Cameos of astonishment on a floodlit stage.

Even then, however, it is not cool, not real,
For into a mold he has mashed colored
Scraps of rubber, and he's melted

The mess into squiggly bugs.
And with them, he's went fishing for praise,
Casting his synthetic, variegated cockroaches
Into the swamp of being harmless,
    Artsy of folksy, bio-
degradable fluff, fodder,
b.s., or to trawl for tenure.
So what if the salty soup of a stew
We have named the sea,
Suddenly, from hither to yon,
Lifts open its locker's lid?

Woeful will be the noise shifting the axis mean:
The cacophony of a thousand billion sounds:
Splashing bones, and jawbones
Clacking,—until coming together
As one, rickety, nightmarish Clack!—
And, while the hollow-socketed
Crews of the ships of all the ages
Beat their scurvied gums that are not there,
From a deeper, unprobed depth,
Strains of a plaintive interlude,
Composed on the spot, will be
Playing second fiddle to the chorus
Of my burnt-sierra ancestors
(Arranged in spoon fashion

In the pot called middle passage),
Quickening from the bottom rot,
Alongside garrisons of goons in spats
Of barnacled logging chains or cement,
Or squished inside of beer kegs or barrels,
As they too offer up their own, despirited,
Damp lament. Yes . . . and if anything then
Beyond the stirring up of this
(when every manner of din and tumult
has gurgled to the surface,

adding its few brittle notes to the cadenza)
Can rival the aforementioned flushing of words,
Lines, and stanzas down the commode, I will be
Too old to blush. I will be too old.

Breathing

Over the hill and through the woods
To where dinners on Sundays were feasts,
And the overfed dog and two cats loved me
For being me, or, more probably,
For just being, and for behaving quite wild.
And so what . . . that the maturation process
Had a habit of sometimes asserting itself,
Involuntarily, by rejecting the hollow kisses
Of an aunt, by leaning away from lips
That must've been two of several gates to the ranch
Where the cowboy lived, whose brand of cancer
Was also his country, his spread.
But didn't everyone know that Dukes of Earl
Were the in-thing for the in-crowd,
Not cattle barons or filter-kings?
And so what . . . that thirteen years doubled
Sees a man despised for not staying thirteen,
Malleable, and someone to be intruded upon
While in the bathroom—as if in dire need
Of a co-conspirator in harvesting
A bumper crop of lint
From the garden of his own navel,
Or instructed in the finer points of hygiene,
Say, how (with a warm washcloth and a bit
Of delicately applied torque) his foreskin
Should be peeled like a banana, his thing washed.
And so what . . . that there was no way, no how,
A sheathe of skin could've grown on him
Since his being diapered by those same pudgy hands.
So, in addition to conditioning himself
To don a mahogany veneer of doofy naivete, he
Taught himself how to discharge a transparent

Lariat of ectoplasm from his navel. Lassoing
The windswept cape of the idea of being
Elsewhere, then jumping astride its back,
He'd leave the confining curse of his body
Suspended—none the wiser that nonresistance,
Inanimation and inertia, was as irresistible to some,
As seductive, as even a bump and a grind.
What an outlandish mechanism the mind is,
Here and there, everywhere, gaining bytes
Of information through the thermal dynamic of osmosis,
Then storing them away in the chitlinlike reservoir
Inside of that fantastic wart
Which the face is a face for. But how like trick
Or treat on Halloween: there are variables
And contingencies—and a child, sooner or later,
Discovers the source of warmth, heat,
And where the best candies are to be had.
Changing costumes, that child returns to that house
For seconds and thirds, or to the spot where the house
Was. As an adult the rationale for this
Rarely, if ever, has anything to do with hunger
Or necessity. Diplomats all, isn't everyone
At least two of a kind with a wild card showing? . . ,
Responding to the lesson 'Never tell
A single living soul' by the numbers,
Saying, with no pun intended, "Tell
What? . . . to whom? . . . about what?" A man
Breathes because he is powerless to do otherwise.

Tug

Not many lifetime guarantees exist.
Yet I might still absolutely become
entranced, primal, a dancing, dizzy riff,
taut then loosened, a syncopated drum.

But if only I can survive the cold,
unawed by the thawed out realities
that shine in from afar, will yesterday's
wishes change into a high-flown castle,
evolving empty but mine to sell or keep . . .

underwritten by bolts of manmade lightning,
numbered at the knees of a steel-gray sky,
defaced, weather-beaten, pitted by time,
ever silent enough to raise the dead,
reborn as shadows going fast asleep.

Shivering now, nearly frozen, am I,
transfixt in front of a dream of myself
atop a white-hot cloud . . . when roused awake,
new as you please, I hear voices screaming
doubts about things not to be said aloud . . .

and then there for just an instant, beating,
never mistaken for shadows or ghosts
daring to sabotage where they are from,
to wit: it is my icy heart come off
upset inside the many sides of me. . . .
Guests, we are, in one riff, one chest, one drum.

University Press of New England publishes books under its own imprint and is the publisher for Brandeis University Press, Brown University Press, University of Connecticut, Dartmouth College, Middlebury College Press, University of New Hampshire, University of Rhode Island, Tufts University, University of Vermont, and Wesleyan University Press.

About the Author

Stephen Todd Booker's poetry has appeared in *Kenyon Review, Seneca Review, Yankee, Cream City Review,* and scores of other journals. He published the chapbook *Waves & license* in 1983 (Greenfield Review Press), and has had poetry anthologized (in *The Light From Another Country,* Greenfield Review Press, 1983), and included in the staged production of the play *Of Cold Places,* in 1988. With poetry forthcoming in publications in Europe, Japan, and South Africa, he currently has two other book manuscripts making the rounds of prospective publishers. Since 1978, when his interest in poetry began, he has lived in and worked from a cell on Florida's death row.

Library of Congress Cataloging-in-Publication Data

Booker, Stephen Todd, 1953–
  Tug / Stephen Todd Booker.
    p. cm. — (Wesleyan poetry)
    ISBN 0-8195-2212-0 (cl.) — ISBN 0-8195-1215-X (pa)
  I. Title. II. Series.
PS3552.O6435T84   1994
811'.54—dc20   94-1306